Grade 2

Improve your piano grade 2!

Paul Harris & Richard Crozier

FABER *ff* MUSIC

© 2014 by Faber Music Ltd
This edition first published in 2014
Bloomsbury House 74–77 Great Russell Street London WC1B 3DA
Music processed by MacMusic
Cover and text designed by Susan Clarke
Printed in England by Caligraving Ltd

ISBN10: 0-571-53882-7
EAN13: 978-0-571-53882-9

To buy Faber Music publications or to find out about the full range of titles available please contact your local music retailer or Faber Music sales enquiries:
Faber Music Ltd, Burnt Mill, Elizabeth Way, Harlow CM20 2HX
Tel: +44 (0) 1279 82 89 82 Fax: +44 (0) 1279 82 89 83
sales@fabermusic.com fabermusicstore.com

Contents

Introduction 4

The Simultaneous Learning map 7

A1 *Impertinence* (Handel) 8

A2 *Minuet in C* (Schale) 12

A3 *Cantabile* (Vanhal) 16

B1 *Sérénade espagnole* (Ferrer) 20

B2 *Lullaby* (Neugasimov) 24

B3 *Gukkuk im Versteck* (Schumann) 28

C1 *I'm an Old Cowhand* (Mercer) 32

C2 *Prelude* (Hummel) 36

C3 *Gachou no Koushin* (Kaneda) 40

Summary 44

Timeline 46

Introduction

This book outlines an interactive, collaborative and imaginative way to teach pieces that have been set for an exam syllabus. The whole philosophy of teaching the Simultaneous Learning way is that we are pro-active rather than reactive. We take the ingredients of a piece and explore them in imaginative ways, making connections between them, being creative and enabling students to learn in a really engaging way. Students should be encouraged to continue with these activities in their practice. Not only do they learn to play the piece, but they can then apply their understanding to learn further pieces more quickly. It is a positive and exciting process that supports thorough learning and the potential for greater progress and continuing achievement.

How to use this book

The work on each piece is divided into three periods:
1 Preliminary work before you introduce the notation;
2 Work when the student is learning the piece from the notation and
3 Refining the piece ready for performance.

The amount of time spent on each period will depend on how students respond to the activities and how quickly they absorb the ingredients and concepts. Many instructions (describe, discuss, identify, explore, etc.) are intended to be carried out collaboratively with the student.

One of the important reasons for adopting Simultaneous Learning is to get away from the 'beginning at bar one and correcting mistakes as they are inevitably made' approach. Instead, we identify the ingredients of each piece, discuss and explore them through imaginative and appropriate activities and by making up (improvising) very simple musical ideas. Through experimentation and mixing and matching the ingredients, students will ultimately learn the pieces in a much more secure and musical way, at the same time deepening their general musical understanding.

Getting started

Play the piece yourself and note the ingredients (they are also listed on each worksheet). Think about the music in terms of each individual student's particular needs and abilities. Look at the suggested activities and decide which ones are most appropriate for the student in that particular lesson, and which order you might like to introduce them. There is no set way to do this – you can begin with whichever you think is best. In the Simultaneous Learning way, if each activity is carefully chosen and each subsequent activity is carefully related and/or sequential, then your student should always achieve. Progress will be natural and ongoing. Do remember that in the first lesson on any new piece (and perhaps for several more lessons, too) the book is better closed and out of sight; try to rely more on your ear, memory and imagination.

Once you start these activities many more will become apparent – simply go with what works and your intuition. Begin anywhere appropriate in each piece – only occasionally at bar 1! Don't always start with the right hand but encourage students to experiment with playing right-hand patterns in the left hand and vice versa. If you have other ideas, do bring them into your teaching: let your imagination take flight! As students gain in confidence, awareness and understanding you can connect these activities with new ones. The dotted lines on each page direct us to the kind of connections we can make as our lessons unfold, and they remind us that all areas of music are linked.

There is no precise amount of time to spend on any particular set of activities and no set order. As you get used to teaching in this way the timing will become second nature. Start by aiming to spend about a third of the lesson on the activities set out on each page (but if you spend an entire lesson on these activities it is time well spent). If the student finds them straightforward then move on – either developing them further or moving on to new ones.

Improvisation is suggested regularly in this book. This doesn't mean jazz improvisation or making up entire pieces. It's about creating little musical fragments, phrases, patterns or exercises using ingredients from the piece. Begin with just one or two notes and move on from there – it's really very simple. Students love this and it brings their learning and understanding of the key elements of a piece to life in a vivid and meaningful way. Develop the habit of improvising regularly – you'll find it a huge help in your teaching.

Call and response is clapping or playing a short phrase to the student, who responds by clapping or playing it back. It's useful for helping students become familiar with new rhythms, dynamics, articulations and so on. **Question and answer** is a little more sophisticated – a short phrase is answered by something slightly different, which complements the musical question. It could be an altered note or rhythm, or a change to the dynamic or articulation. Both are simple, enjoyable and creative activities that develop understanding in a musical way.

For students using this book (with or without a teacher)

This may be the first time you have used the Simultaneous Learning approach. Rather than simply 'playing through the piece', using these activities will encourage you to explore and experiment and really get to know the music thoroughly. The advantage of working this way is that you should find it much easier to apply the principles from one piece to another. Time spent 'off the piece', working with its ingredients, should prove much more valuable than simply playing straight through. Learning by copying your teacher may have its place, but it is a short-term strategy and will not ultimately help you to develop and become a confident, independent musician.

The Simultaneous Learning map

The Simultaneous Learning Map is a graphic representation of what we as musicians and teachers instinctively know. The map depicts the various areas of music and the fact that they all connect. This representation is not entirely accurate as of course all the areas connect. Most teachers and students will wish the teaching to be based around a piece or song, so that is placed in the centre. Just how we move around the map will be determined by a combination of teacher experience, how the student is responding and how the lesson is unfolding. The beauty of Simultaneous Learning and its map is that there are infinite possibilities. Teachers can make the process their own.

For more detail on this see *Simultaneous Learning: The definitive guide* (Faber Music).

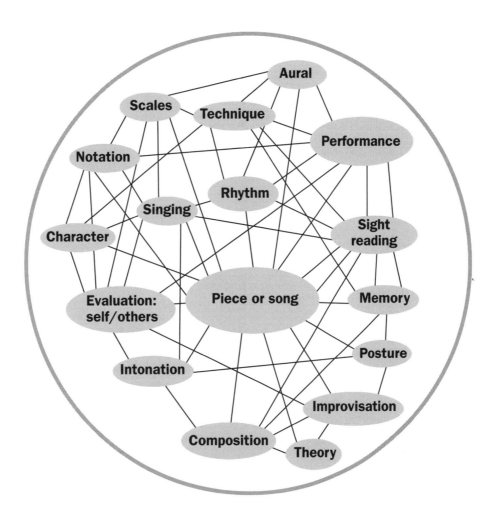

Impertinence (Handel)

All about … terraced dynamics, independent hands and a confident sound

Pre-notation activities

Rhythm

- Discuss the ¢ time signature and its various names (simple duple time, cut common, $\frac{2}{2}$ and *alla breve*).
- Choose and clap a suitable pulse in ¢.
- Play call-and-response clapping games using two-bar phrases:

Dynamics

- Play a G minor scale (hands separately and together) and arpeggio:
  - *mp*, *mf* and *f*
  - Experiment with each hand playing at a different dynamic level.
- Play call-and-response games using short phrases in ¢ from the piece, exploring these dynamics.

Key and scale patterns

- Play the scale and arpeggio of G minor hands separately and together from notation and from memory.
- Play the scale (or part of the scale) using this rhythm on each note:

Theory

- Discuss what ¢ means and try to find out how the symbol evolved.
- Discuss and practise trills on various notes in the key of G minor. Why are trills a feature of this music?
- What is a sequence? Make up a short and simple pattern and play it sequentially on each note of the ascending scale of G minor.

Aural

- Listen to a performance of *Impertinence* and identify whether it is in two or three time.
- Discuss whether the piece sounds minor or major.
- Clap the pulse as you listen to the performance, emphasising the strong beat of the bar.

Title, character and context

- This is a bourrée, so explore this dance and the harpsichord.
- Listen to a harpsichord.
- In the 17th century the word 'impertinent' meant being rather bold. Do you think that might describe the character of this piece?

Introducing the notation (opening the book)

Rhythm and pulse

- Set up a ₵ pulse. Play two bars (hands separately or together), then count and hear the two bars internally. Play the next two bars and so on.
- Find any rhythmic patterns that appear in both hands.
- Clap the rhythm of the right and left hands with someone as a duet; swap parts.
- Try tapping the rhythm of both hands together, section by section.

Dynamics

- Explore the idea of 'terraced' dynamics (a Baroque style), as suggested by the editor.
- Make up a piece which explores terraced dynamics.
- Circle all the dynamics using different colours for the different levels.

Aural

- Sing back two-bar phrases from the piece.
- Play a phrase from the piece twice. The second time, make a change for the student to identify.

Special ingredients

- Discuss and play some *staccato* minims (bar 7). Improvise some music to explore them.
- Practise the left-hand octave jumps in bars 17 and 19. Make up some phrases in the left hand using octaves.
- Trills usually come at the end of phrases. Make up some music that uses trills.
- Identify the sequences in *Impertinence* (bars 9–12 and 13–14).

Key and scale patterns*

- Discuss the key of the piece and play the scale and arpeggio regularly.
- Identify any accidentals and discuss why they are there.
- Explore the scales and arpeggios of keys related to G minor: B flat major and D major and minor. Discuss their relationship.

Title, character and context

- Find out some facts about Handel.
- Remembering this was written for a harpsichord, play some patterns in G minor in both hands using a clean and clearly separated articulation.
- Try to find a bourrée being danced online.

* For more help with scales and arpeggios, try the G minor Finger Fitness section in *Improve your scales!* Grade 2.

Playing and refining the piece

Rhythm and pulse

- Tap the rhythm of both hands together with a metronome providing the minim pulse.
- Explore playing the piece at different speeds and discuss which sounds best.
- Sing one line while clapping the other.

Key and scale patterns

- Regularly play the scales and arpeggios of G minor, D minor and D major in a confident style at the tempo of the piece. Try to imitate the sound of a harpsichord.
- Sight-read a piece in G minor.*

Aural

- Regularly try to hear the piece internally – just the rhythm at first, then the melody too.
- Visualise your hands playing the piece at the same time as hearing it internally.
- Without looking at the music, describe the dynamic shape of *Impertinence*.

Articulation and dynamics

- Play sections concentrating on really clear articulation. Are the contrasts between slurred and articulated notes really obvious?
- Try shaping the phrases (even within the terraced dynamics) with small *crescendos* and *diminuendos*.

Title and context

- At the start there is almost a canon between the right and left hands. Find out about musical canons and make up a simple one.
- Listen to other pieces for harpsichord by Handel.
- Think about the character – does the music dance along?

Performing

- Start performing the piece all the way through, hands separately as well as together.
- Try to memorise the piece.
- Perform the whole piece to relatives and friends and/or make a recording.

* For related sight-reading pieces try *Improve Your Sight-reading!* Grade 2.

Student's worksheet

Impertinence ingredients

Key signature G minor

Other scale patterns
  B flat major

Time signature ¢

Rhythms

Dynamics *mp mf f*

Articulation *Staccato*
  minims, slurs, clearly
  separated notes
  (harpsichord-like)

Character Dance-like,
  march-like, serious

Form Binary

Special features Sequences,
  trills, terraced dynamics

Terms and signs
  Allegro ♩ = c.84

☐ Explore these ingredients by making up little musical patterns, exercises or phrases.
Mix and match them where you can. Tick each ingredient when you've used it.

☐ Sight-read this piece and list its main ingredients here:

Allegro

☐ Write out the first four bars of the piece (both hands), including all terms and signs:

- What does *Allegro* mean? _____

- What does ¢ mean? _____

- Circle the first time the fifth degree of the scale appears in this passage in each hand.

- How many times does the rhythm in bar 3 of the right hand recur in the piece? _____

- How many times does the rhythm in bar 4 of the left hand recur in the piece? _____

- Play this section from your notation.

Minuet in C (Shale)

All about ... elegance, balance between the hands and crisp ornaments

Pre-notation activities

Rhythm and pulse

- Choose and clap a suitable pulse in $\frac{3}{4}$: firstly clapping all beats, then one person claps beat 1 and the other beats 2 and 3. Swap around. Feel the different 'weight' of the beats.

- Play call-and-response clapping games using two-bar phrases from the piece such as:

  and then longer four-bar phrases.

- Using the same pulse, explore ♩. ♪ and ♪. ♪ rhythms by making up little tunes.

Dynamics

- Play a C major scale and arpeggio:
    - *mp*, *mf* and *f*
    - with a *crescendo* ascending and *diminuendo* descending
- Play call-and-response games using short phrases in $\frac{3}{4}$ from the piece, exploring these dynamics.

Theory

- Introduce the idea of sequences and make up some simple sequential phrases.
- Explore mordents and make up some exercises using them.

Aural

- Listen to a performance of *Minuet in C*.
- Clap the pulse as you listen to the performance, emphasising the strong beat in the bar.

Title, character and context

- Find out about what a minuet is and listen to this (or any other) minuet.
- Find out about how a minuet was danced.

Key and scale patterns

- Play the scale and arpeggio of C major from notation and from memory.
- Record this bass line and improvise over it using the notes of the C major scale. Add chords to the notes if you like.

Introducing the notation (opening the book)

Rhythm and pulse

- Set up a $\frac{3}{4}$ pulse. Play two bars (hands separately or together), then count and hear the two bars internally. Play the next two bars and so on.
- Find and clap any recurring rhythmic patterns.
- Clap the rhythms of the right and left hands with someone as a duet; swap parts.
- Tap out the rhythms from the notation. Continue until the rhythm of both hands can be tapped together.

Dynamics

- Apply the dynamic levels to scale and arpeggio patterns.
- Notice how the various dynamic levels fit the phrases. Look at these in the music and look for where you might add more.
- Circle all the dynamics using different colours for the different levels.

Aural

- Play two-bar phrases (at a suitable pitch) and sing them back.
- Play a phrase from the piece twice. The second time, make a change for the student to identify.

Key and scale patterns*

- Discuss the key of the piece and play the scale and arpeggio regularly.
- Identify any accidentals and discuss why they are there.
- Explore the scales and arpeggios of keys related to C major: G and F major and A minor. Discuss their relationship.

Special ingredients

- There are many octave jumps in this piece – lots of left-hand practice is needed. Try memorising the left hand, as well as playing without looking at the hands.
- Identify the one jump of a ninth. Make up a short piece to explore this.
- Find the sequence and then continue it for two more bars.

Title, character and context

- Compose a short minuet in C based on the ingredients of this piece.
- Listen to some other Baroque minuets and try dancing to them.
- Find out something about Frederick the Great, the musical king for whom this piece was probably written.

* For more help with scales and broken chords, try the C major Finger Fitness section in *Improve your scales!* Grade 2.

Playing and refining the piece

Key and scale patterns

- Regularly play the scale and arpeggio of C and G majors in an elegant, minuet-like style in three time.
- Try playing a contrary motion C major scale.
- Sight-read a piece in C major.*

Rhythm and pulse

- Explore playing the pieces at different speeds. Discuss which tempo sounds the most dance-like.
- Tap the rhythm of the whole piece with both hands at the same time.

Special ingredients

- Practise the mordents separately, at the various dynamics of the piece. Make up some music that includes the mordent shapes and ensure there are no unnecessary accents that spoil the musical line and flow of the music.
- Focus on the balance of the hands and ultimately on the right hand singing out over the left.

Aural

- Regularly try to hear the piece internally – just the rhythm at first, then the melody too.
- Visualise yourself fingering the piece at the same time as hearing it internally.
- Without looking at the music, describe the dynamic shape of *Minuet in C*.

Performing

- Think about the character – imagine you are accompanying the dancing in an 18th-century ball.
- Try to memorise the piece.
- Perform the whole piece to relatives and friends and/or make a recording.

* For related sight-reading pieces try *Improve Your Sight-reading!* Grade 2.

Student's worksheet

Minuet in C ingredients

Key signature C major

Other scale patterns G major

Time signature 3/4

Rhythms

♩. ♪ ♫♫♩♩ ♩ |

♫♩ ♩ |♫♫♩ ⁊ |

Dynamics *mp*, *mf*, *f*

Articulation Clearly separated notes, slurred groups

Character Dance-like, elegant, charming

Form Binary

Special features Mordents, sequences, hand balance, left-hand leaps

Terms and signs ♩ = c.112, 1st & 2nd time bars

☐ Explore these ingredients by making up little musical patterns, exercises or phrases. Mix and match them where you can. Tick each ingredient when you've used it.

☐ Write these tonic triads, with the correct key signature each time:

C major   G major   A minor   A major

☐ Write out the first four bars of the left hand:

- Describe the interval between first and second notes: _____
- Put a bracket over any more of the same interval.
- Write the name under each note.

☐ Complete a four-bar rhythm from this opening. Then clap it and make up a melody to fit your rhythm.

Cantabile (Vanhal)

All about ... a sweet, singing sound, neat accompaniment and warm cadences

Pre-notation activities

Rhythm

- Discuss the ¢ time signature and its various names (simple duple time, cut common, $\frac{2}{2}$ and *alla breve*).
- Choose and clap a suitable pulse in ¢.
- Play call-and-response clapping games using two-bar phrases, such as:

Dynamics

- Play a G major scale and arpeggio:
  - *p* and *f* with a *dolce* tone
  - with a *crescendo* ascending and *diminuendo* descending.

Key and scale patterns

- Play the scale and arpeggio of G major from notation and from memory.
- Make up some music in this key – perhaps hold or play repeated Gs in the left hand while improvising a song-like tune in the right.
- Improvise some phrases in G major exploring *fz*, *staccato*, gently separated notes and slurs.

Theory

- Find out what *cantabile*, *dolce* and *fz* mean.
- Discuss and explore how turns work.
- Compose a bar of music in ¢ time and then use it as a basis for a short improvisation.

Title, character and context

- Investigate Alberti bass and when it was popular.
- Listen to other pieces with Alberti-bass accompaniments. Which composers used this?

Aural

- Listen to a performance of *Cantabile*.
- Clap the pulse as you listen to the performance, emphasising the strong beat in the bar.
- Discuss the dynamics in the piece: are the changes sudden or gradual?

Introducing the notation (opening the book)

Rhythm

- Set up a ¢ pulse. Play two bars (hands separately or together), then count and hear the two bars internally. Play the next two bars and so on.

- Compare bars 1, 5, 10 and 11. How are these rhythms similar and different? Make up a tune based on these rhythms.

- Clap the rhythm of this piece from the notation until secure, hands separately at first and then (section by section) hands together.

- Discuss and explore the different upbeats.

Dynamics

- Explore how you can use *crescendo* and *diminuendo* to shape the opening phrase. Experiment with other phrases in the same way.

- Circle all the dynamics using different colours for the different levels.

Aural

- Sing back two-bar phrases from the piece (at a suitable octave).

- Play a phrase from the piece twice. The second time, make a change for the student to identify.

Key and scale patterns*

- Discuss the key of the piece and play the scale and arpeggio regularly.

- Identify any accidentals and discuss why they are there.

- Find any patterns in *Cantabile* that are based on the G major scale and arpeggio and practise them carefully.

- Explore the scales and arpeggios of keys related to G major: D major and E minor. Discuss their relationship.

Special ingredients

- Learn the two chords patterns in bars 8 and 12 by heart. Experiment with playing them with different dynamics.

- Learn the last four bars of the piece by heart. Make sure you maintain the *piano* dynamic.

Title, character and context

- Discuss the title.

- Think of some words to describe the character of *Cantabile*.

- When was this music written? Listen to other music of this period.

* For more help with scales and arpeggios, try the G major Finger Fitness section in *Improve your scales!* Grade 2.

Playing and refining the piece

Rhythm and pulse

- Explore playing the piece at different speeds.
- Tap the rhythm of the whole piece with both hands at the same time and the pulse with your foot.

Scales and arpeggios

- Play the scales and arpeggios of G and D major and E minor in a smooth, expressive and elegant manner.
- Sight-read a piece in G major.*

Aural

- Regularly try to hear the piece internally – just the rhythm at first, then the melody too.
- Visualise yourself fingering the piece at the same time as hearing it internally.

Phrasing and dynamics

- Circle all the dynamics using different colours for the different levels.
- Try singing phrases from the piece, at whichever octave is most comfortable. Then play the piece, phrase by phrase, giving it the same phrasing, shape and character.

Title, character and context

- Can you imagine this piece as TV or film music? What sort of scene could it accompany?
- Focus on playing with an expressive, gentle flowing character.

Performing

- Explore hand balance and the effect of different volume levels in each hand. Record these experiments and listen carefully.
- Try to memorise the piece.
- Perform the whole piece to relatives and friends and/or make a recording.

* For related sight-reading pieces try *Improve Your Sight-reading!* Grade 2.

Student's worksheet

Cantabile ingredients

Key signature G major

Other scale patterns
Chromatic, D major

Time signature ¢

Dynamics *p*, *f*, *fz*

Rhythms

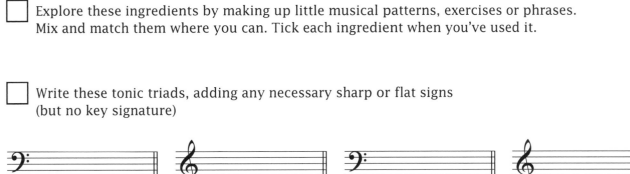

Articulation Gently separated
notes, slurs, *staccato*

Character Expressive, song-
like, gentle, flowing

Form Ternary-like with coda

Special features Alberti bass,
turns

Terms and signs *Cantabile,
dolce*, ♩ = c.56

☐ Explore these ingredients by making up little musical patterns, exercises or phrases.
Mix and match them where you can. Tick each ingredient when you've used it.

☐ Write these tonic triads, adding any necessary sharp or flat signs
(but no key signature)

G major   D major   A major   E minor

☐ Sight-read this piece and list its main ingredients here:

☐ Complete a four-bar rhythm using this opening. Then clap it and make up
a melody to fit your rhythm.

Sérénade espagnole (Ferrer)

All about ... a Spanish flavour, crisp articulation and guitars

Pre-notation activities

Rhythm

- Discuss $\frac{3}{8}$ and look at (or write) some simple tunes in this time signature.
- Choose and clap a suitable pulse in $\frac{3}{8}$.
- Play call-and-response clapping games using many rhythmic shapes from the piece, such as:

Aural

- Listen to a performance of *Sérénade espagnole*.
- Clap the pulse as you listen to the performance, emphasising the strong beat in the bar. Listen for any changes of tempo and discuss.
- Discuss the dynamics in the piece: are the changes sudden or gradual?

Dynamics

- Play an A minor scale and arpeggio:
  - *p* and *mf*
  - with a *crescendo* ascending and *diminuendo* descending.

Key and scale patterns

- Play the scale and arpeggio of A minor from notation and from memory.
- Play the scale (or part of the scale) using rhythms from the piece, such as:

- Try fitting into an arpeggio pattern.

Articulation

- Use the notes of the chord (triad or arpeggio) of A minor and make up some tunes using the following articulations:
  - *staccato*
  - accents
  - slurs

  Work with both hands.

Title, character and context

- Listen to some Spanish guitar music and think about the rhythmic drive, melodic characteristics and different sounds in the performance.

Introducing the notation (opening the book)

Rhythm and pulse

- Set up a suitable pulse in $\frac{3}{8}$. Play two bars (hands separately or together), then count and hear the two bars internally. Play the next two bars and so on.

- Find and clap any recurring rhythmic patterns.

- Compare the rhythms in bars 13–14 with bars 29–30. Clap both until completely secure.

- Clap the rhythm of *Sérénade espagnole* from the notation until secure, hands separately at first and then (section by section) hands together.

Dynamics

- Discuss the short *crescendo – diminuendo* in bars 3–4, 7–8 and so on. Make up some other patterns to explore this.

- Circle all the dynamics using different colours for the different levels.

- Play an A minor scale and arpeggio *p* and *f*, with this rhythm on each note:

Aural

- Sing back two-bar phrases from the piece.

- Play a phrase from the piece twice. The second time, make a change for the student to identify.

Special features

- Play the scale and arpeggio of A minor, experimenting with accenting different notes.

- Play the scale and arpeggio with a light, Spanish guitar-like touch.

- Explore *acciaccaturas* and improvise some music using them.

- Discuss the spread-chord marking in bars 10, 12, 26 and 28 and make up some music using this idea.

Key and scale patterns*

- Discuss the key of the piece and play the scale and arpeggio regularly.

- Identify any accidentals and discuss why they are there.

- Explore the scales and arpeggios of keys related to A minor: C major and E minor. Discuss their relationship.

- Look at the opening two bars of the left hand and discuss how these relate to the A minor triad. Play these bars repeatedly and improvise a right-hand tune over them.

Title, character and context

- What features of Spanish guitar music are in this piece?

- Make up a short, Spanish guitar-like piece of your own, using ingredients from the piece.

* For more help with scales and arpeggios, try the A minor Finger Fitness section in *Improve your scales!* Grade 2.

Playing and refining the piece

Rhythm and pulse

- Tap the rhythm of the left and right hands together.

- Make up your own tune to fit over the left hand, bars 1–8.

- Explore playing the piece at different speeds and consider which gives the most authentic Spanish flavour.

Scale and arpeggio

- Play the scales and arpeggios of A and E minors and C major with a Spanish guitar-like sound and articulation.

- Sight-read a piece in A minor.*

Aural

- Regularly try to hear the piece internally – just the rhythm at first, then the melody too.

- Visualise yourself fingering the piece at the same time as hearing it internally.

Dynamics

- Explore the *mf* markings and consider where it might be musical to take the dynamic level up to *f*.

- Think about shaping of all the phrases, using *crescendo* and *diminuendo*.

Performing

- Focus on playing this piece with a Spanish guitar-like sound. Check this is brought out vividly in performance.

- Try to memorise the piece.

- Perform the whole piece to relatives and friends and/or make a recording.

Title, character and context

- Does this piece suggest a picture or a story? Find an image or draw a picture that suits it.

- Explore hand balance and the effect of different volume levels in each hand. Record these experiments and listen carefully.

* For related sight-reading pieces try *Improve Your Sight-reading!* Grade 2.

Student's worksheet

Sérénade espagnole ingredients

Key signature A minor

Other scale patterns
E minor, C major

Time signature $\frac{3}{8}$

Rhythms

Dynamics *p* *mf*

Articulation
Staccato, accents, slurs

Character Spanish guitar,
dance-like, light

Form A A'

Special features
Left-hand accompaniment
figures, *acciaccaturas* and
spread chords

Terms and signs
Comodo, poco rit, a tempo,
♩. = c.56

☐ Explore these ingredients by making up little musical patterns, exercises or phrases.
Mix and match them where you can. Tick each ingredient when you've used it.

☐ Write out an A minor scale in semibreves in the right hand, ascending and descending.
Include a clef, key signature and any accidentals that are necessary:

☐ Sight-read this piece and list its main ingredients here:

Andante

☐ Fill in the correct rest at the places marked * to complete each bar:

☐ Give the meaning of these:

- *Comodo* _____
- *mf* _____

- *Poco rit.* _____
- *A tempo* _____

Lullaby (Neugasimov)

All about ... long flowing phrases, a gentle sound and beautiful, *pianissimo* chords at the end

Pre-notation activities

Rhythm

- Discuss $\frac{6}{8}$ and look at (or write) some simple tunes in this time signature.

- Choose and clap a suitable pulse in $\frac{6}{8}$: one person claps ♩. ♩. while the other claps quavers. Then swap around.

- Play call-and-response clapping games using two-bar phrases such as:

  and

  When these are secure try longer four-bar phrases, such as:

Dynamics

- Play a C major scale and arpeggio:
  - *pp, p, mf*
  - with a *crescendo* and *diminuendo*.

- Improvise a short C major piece in $\frac{6}{8}$ using these dynamic markings, with one hand or hands together.

Articulation

- Make up some melodies in C major using:
  - slurs
  - gently separated notes
  - *tenuto*.

- Play call-and-response games using short phrases from the piece, exploring these articulations.

Key and scale patterns

- Play the scale and arpeggio of C major from notation and from memory.

- Introduce the left-hand arpeggio pattern in bar 1. Repeat it while improvising a right-hand tune using the notes of the scale.

Title, character and context

- What is a lullaby? Listen to other lullabies.

- Listen to Brahms' *Lullaby*.

- List the main characteristics of a lullaby.

Aural

- Listen to a performance of *Lullaby*.

- Clap the pulse as you listen to the performance, emphasising the strong beat in the bar.

- Discuss the dynamics in the piece: are the changes sudden or gradual?

Introducing the notation (opening the book)

Rhythm and pulse

- Set up a suitable pulse in $\frac{6}{8}$. Play two bars (hands separately or together), then count and hear the two bars internally. Play the next two bars and so on.

- How many times does the rhythm of the opening four-bar right-hand phrase return? Clap this rhythm from the notation a few times and then from memory.

- Tap the rhythm of *Lullaby* from the notation until secure, hands separately at first and then (section by section) hands together.

Dynamics and phrasing

- Work at the left hand, putting in all the dynamics but keeping it smooth. Practise it with different rhythms (such as dotted patterns).

- Experiment with the opening four-bar phrase, taking care to shape it with a *crescendo* and *diminuendo*.

- Circle all the dynamics with appropriate colours.

- Discuss how the piece is split into regular four-bar phrases except for the final section.

Aural

- Sing back phrases from the piece at an appropriate octave.

- Play a phrase from the piece twice. The second time, make a change for the student to identify.

Special ingredients

- Discuss the tied notes and how they will be counted.

- How does the opening right-hand phrase compare with the second phrase?

- Improvise a right-hand melody that includes octaves leaps and *tenutos*. Add dynamics from the piece.

- Explore the chords in the final bars. Look carefully at which notes make up each chord.

Key and scale patterns*

- Review the key of the piece and play the scale and arpeggio regularly, keeping the right hand more prominent than the left.

- Identify any accidentals and discuss why they are there.

- Explore the scales and arpeggios of keys related to C major: G major and A minor. Discuss their relationship.

Title, character and context

- Write down some words to describe the character.

- Consider how to develop the lullaby character of this piece.

* For more help with scales and arpeggios, try the C major Finger Fitness section in *Improve your scales!* Grade 2.

Playing and refining the piece

Rhythm and pulse

- Explore playing the piece at different speeds. Discuss which sounds best: what are the advantages of playing it slower and faster?
- Experiment with a small *rit.* before the return of the tune at bar 17.
- Tap the rhythm of both hands at the same time whilst tapping a dotted-crotchet pulse with a foot.

Scale and arpeggio

- Play the scales and arpeggios of C and G majors and A minor with a *legato*, lullaby-like feel.
- Try playing a contrary motion C major scale with a lullaby character.
- Sight-read a piece in C major.*

Aural

- Regularly try to hear the piece internally – just the rhythm at first, then the melody too.
- Visualise yourself fingering the piece at the same time as hearing it internally.
- Clap the pulse of other pieces in compound time, identifying whether they are in two or three time.

Articulation and dynamics

- Play the piece *staccato* and discuss how it sounds.
- Play the piece reversing all the dynamic levels and discuss the difference.
- Then play *Lullaby* as directed in the notation.

Title, character and context

- Discuss the character of *Lullaby* – does it suggest a picture, story or particular mood?
- Do the octave leaps suggest anything? What happens at the end?

Performing

- Explore hand balance and the effect of different volume levels in each hand. Record these experiments and listen carefully.
- Try to memorise the piece.
- Perform the whole piece to relatives and friends and/or make a recording.

* For related sight-reading pieces try *Improve Your Sight-reading!* Grade 2.

Student's worksheet

Lullaby ingredients

Key signature C major

Related scale patterns
G major, A minor

Time signature $\frac{6}{8}$

Rhythms

Dynamics *pp p mf*
cresc., dim. ◁ ▷

Articulation *Legato,
tenuto*

Character Gentle,
flowing, a lullaby

Special features Octaves,
triadic accompaniment
figures, chords

Form Ternary, plus
short coda

Terms and signs
*Comodo e cantabile, molto
legato,* ♩. = c.63

☐ Explore these ingredients by making up little musical patterns, exercises or phrases.
Mix and match them where you can. Tick each ingredient when you've used it.

☐ Write out both hands of the first four bars of the piece. Include all terms and signs:

- What does *comodo e cantabile* mean? _____
- What does *molto legato* mean? _____
- Put a star over the right-hand note which is the sixth degree of the scale.
- Put a star under the left-hand note which is the second degree of the scale.
- Then play this section from your notation.

☐ Sight-read this piece and list its main ingredients here:

Gently

mp

☐ Complete a four-bar rhythm using this opening. Then clap it and make up
a melody to fit your rhythm.

Gukkuk im Versteck (Schumann)

All about ... story-telling, really precise rhythm and remaining *pianissimo* throughout

Pre-notation activities

Rhythm

- Choose and clap a suitable pulse in $\frac{2}{4}$, with a stronger clap on the first beat of the bar.
- Play call-and-response clapping games using rhythms from the piece:

Focus on feeling the rests clearly.

Key and scale patterns

- Play the scale and broken chord of F major from notation and from memory.
- Play the triads of C major, A minor, G minor and D minor. Improvise using these chords.

Aural

- Listen to a performance of *Gukkuk im Versteck*.
- Clap the pulse as you listen to the performance, emphasising the strong beat in the bar.
- Discuss the dynamics and articulation in the piece: how do they help to create the character?

Dynamics and phrasing

- Play an F major scale and broken chord:
  - *pp*
  - with a *crescendo* ascending and *diminuendo* descending, then reverse.
- The dynamic throughout is *pp*; experiment with a slightly broader range of dynamics to give shape to the phrases, always keeping the quiet feel.

Articulation

- Play a slow scale of F major, one hand *staccato*, the other *legato*. Begin with just one octave and extend when confident.
- Improvise some F major music in $\frac{2}{4}$ using shapes and ingredients from the piece.

Title, character and context

- Make up a little piece that describes a children's game.
- Make up some *pianissimo* music that conveys a chase.

Introducing the notation (opening the book)

Rhythm and pulse

- Set up a suitable pulse in $\frac{2}{4}$. Play two bars (hands separately or together), then count and hear the two bars internally. Play the next two bars and so on.
- Find and clap any recurring rhythmic patterns.
- Clap the rhythm of *Gukkuk im Versteck* from the notation until secure, hands separately at first and then (section by section) hands together.

Dynamics and phrasing

- Explore playing chords *pianissimo* and also work at *staccato*, *pianissimo* semiquaver groups. Use patterns from the piece or make up simple patterns.
- Practise adding little dynamic changes to shape the short phrases, but always keeping *pianissimo*.

Special ingredients

- Improvise a piece where both hands are playing in unison.
- Improvise a little piece called 'Hide and seek', with silent pauses between notes as well as pauses on notes or chords.

Aural

- Play call-and-response and question-and-answer clapping games with two- and four-bar phrases from the piece.
- Clap along with the pulse of other pieces in $\frac{2}{4}$, emphasising the stronger first beat of the bar.
- Play a phrase from the piece twice. The second time, make a change for the student to identify.

Key and scale patterns*

- Review the key of the piece and play the scale and broken chord regularly *pianissimo* and *staccato*.
- Identify the accidentals and discuss why they are there.
- Find patterns based on the scale and chords of F major and C major. Find chords of G minor and D minor, too.
- Explore the scales sand arpeggios of keys related to F major: C major and D minor. Discuss their relationship.

Title, character and context

- Discuss the title.
- Work out a story to fit the music.
- Find out some facts about Schumann.

* For more help with scales and broken chords, try the F major Finger Fitness section in *Improve your scales!* Grade 2.

Playing and refining the piece

Rhythm and pulse

- Explore playing the piece at different speeds, bearing in mind the control necessary to play the semiquavers.
- Tap a pulse and hear the rhythm of the right-hand part in your head.
- Tap the rhythm of both lines at the same time.

Scale and arpeggio

- Regularly play the scales and broken chord or arpeggios of F major, C major and D minor *pianissimo* and *staccato*.
- Sight-read pieces in F major and D minor.*

Aural

- Regularly try to hear the piece internally – just the rhythm at first, then the melody too.
- Visualise yourself fingering the piece at the same time as hearing it internally.
- Discuss the dynamics and articulation of *Gukkuk im Versteck*.

Articulation and dynamics

- Play sections concentrating on the contrast between the slurred and *staccato* notes within phrases.
- Then add dynamics to give the piece its phrasing, shape and character.

Title, character and context

- Describe the character of the different sections of *Gukkuk im Versteck*.
- Listen to other music from *Album for the Young* by Schumann.

Performing

- Focus on the cheeky, lively character and the excitement of the game when playing *Gukkuk im Versteck*.
- Try to memorise the piece.
- Perform the whole piece to relatives and friends and/or make a recording.

* For related sight-reading pieces try *Improve Your Sight-reading!* Grade 2.

Student's worksheet

Gukkuk im Versteck ingredients

Key signature F major

Other scale patterns
D minor, C major

Time signature 2/4

Rhythms

Dynamics *pp* throughout

Articulation Slurred and *staccato*

Character Excitement, secrecy, mischievous, cheeky

Special ingredient Playing in unison, pauses, rests

Form Binary with some repetition of the opening

Terms and signs *Immer sehr leise* (always very soft), pause, 1st and 2nd time bars, ♩ = c.84

☐ Explore these ingredients by making up little musical patterns, exercises or phrases. Mix and match them where you can. Tick each ingredient when you've used it.

☐ Sight-read this piece and list its main ingredients here:

Like a march

☐ Write out the tonic triads of C major, F major, E minor and D minor, adding the correct key signatures each time:

☐ Write out all the rests which appear in *Gukkuk im Versteck*, with the equivalent note value alongside each:

☐ Complete a four-bar rhythm using this opening. Then clap it and make up a melody to fit your rhythm.

I'm an Old Cowhand (Mercer)

All about ... a sense of fun, relaxed swing and cowboys

Pre-notation activities

Rhythm

- Choose and clap a suitable pulse in $\frac{4}{4}$, emphasising the first beat of the bar.
- Introduce and discuss swing rhythm and compare it with 'straight' quavers. Do lots of call-and-response clapping exercises.
- Play call-and-response clapping games using rhythms from the piece:

Dynamics

- Play an F major scale and broken chord using the following dynamics:
  - *mf, f*
  - with *crescendo* ascending and *diminuendo* descending.

Aural

- Listen to a performance of *I'm an Old Cowhand*.
- Clap the pulse as you listen to the performance, emphasising the strong beat in the bar.
- Discuss the dynamics and articulation. Are there any accents?

Key and scale patterns

- Play the scale and broken chord of F major from notation and from memory. Try it using swing rhythm.
- Work out the tonic triad of F major.
- Play the arpeggios of D and A minors and work out these tonic triads, too.

Title, character and context

- Listen to Bing Crosby sing the original *I'm an Old Cowhand* song.
- Listen to songs such as *In the Mood* and *Don't Get Around Much Anymore* to get used to swung rhythms.
- Watch a Western, paying particular attention to the music.

Special ingredients

- Discuss syncopation.
- Play call-and-response games using short phrases from the piece.
- Keep playing bars 1–2 until memorised, then improvise some right-hand music above it. Begin with just semibreve Fs and develop from there.

Introducing the notation (opening the book)

Rhythm

- Find and clap any recurring rhythmic patterns.
- Clap the rhythm of the right and left hands with someone as a duet; swap parts.
- Tap the rhythm of *I'm an Old Cowhand* from the notation until secure, hands separately at first and then (section by section) hands together.

Aural

- Sing back some two-bar phrases from the piece at an appropriate octave.
- Play a phrase from the piece twice. The second time, make a change for the student to identify.

Special ingredients

- Look at the chords on the third beat of bars 18, 20 and 22. Improvise using the notes of these chords.
- Identify syncopated rhythms in *I'm an Old Cowhand* and explore the rhythms through improvisation.
- Look at the right-hand bars made up of thirds (bars 19 and 21) and practise them by making up a short exercise.

Dynamics and articulation

- Explore playing a *crescendo* through one bar using patterns in F major and $\frac{4}{4}$. Choose dynamics which allow good contrasts to be made.
- Choose a phrase that is marked with lots of articulation directions and explore it, making the articulations really vivid.

Title, character and context

- Discuss the title and what a cowhand does.
- Choose some imaginative words to describe the character of this music.
- Work out where the words 'yippee i oh ti-ay' fit the music and how they help with the swing rhythm.

Scale and key patterns*

- Discuss the key of the piece play the scale and broken chord.
- Identify any accidentals and discuss why they are there.
- Explore the scales and arpeggios of keys related to F major: C major and D minor. Discuss their relationship and find any patterns based on these scales and chords in the piece.

* For more help with scales and broken chords, try the F major Finger Fitness section in *Improve your scales!* Grade 2.

Playing and refining the piece

Rhythm and pulse

- Explore playing the piece at different speeds. Discuss which tempo captures the mood best.
- Tap a pulse and hear the rhythm of both parts in your head.
- Tap the rhythm of both lines at the same time.
- Learn another piece with swung quavers, or trying swinging the quavers in known pieces.

Scales and key

- Regularly play the scales and broken chord or arpeggios of F major, C major and D minor with a swing rhythm on each note:
- Sight-read pieces in F major and D minor.*

Special ingredients

- Work on the passage at bars 13–16. Connect with different speeds, articulations and dynamics to improve this phrase. Do the same with bars 19–20.

Aural

- Regularly try to hear the piece internally – just the rhythm at first, then the melody too.
- Visualise yourself fingering the piece at the same time as hearing it internally.
- Learn to sing the original song.

Title, character and context

- Make up a cowboy piece using as many ingredients from this piece as possible.
- Write a story or draw (or find) a picture about this piece.

Performing

- Focus on the laid-back, cheerful cowboy character when playing *I'm an Old Cowhand*.
- Try to memorise the piece.
- Perform the whole piece to relatives and friends and/or make a recording.

* For related sight-reading pieces try *Improve Your Sight-reading!* Grade 2.

Student's worksheet

I'm an Old Cowhand ingredients

Key signature F major

Other scale patterns D minor

Time signature $\frac{4}{4}$

Rhythms Swung quavers

Dynamics *mf f*

Articulation *Staccato*, different kinds of accentuated notes

Character Cowboy song, laid-back, jazzy

Form Free, with some repetition

Special ingredients Swing rhythm, riffs, thirds, syncopation

Terms and signs Grace note, ♩ = c.120

☐ Explore these ingredients by making up little musical patterns, exercises or phrases. Mix and match them where you can. Tick each ingredient when you've used it.

☐ Write out an ascending left-hand scale of F major with any sharps or flats necessary (no key signature):

☐ Sight-read this piece and list its main ingredients here:

With lots of energy

☐ Write out bars 19–22 of the piece, both hands, including all terms and signs:

- How many times does the third degree of the scale appear in the right hand? _____
- Circle the second degree of the scale in the left hand the first time it appears.
- Which right-hand bar contains only the notes of a D minor triad? _____
- Play it from your notation.

Prelude (Hummel)

All about... arpeggio figures, contrasting articulation and a surprise ending

Pre-notation activities

Rhythm and pulse

- Choose and clap a suitable pulse in $\frac{2}{4}$, emphasising the first beat of the bar.
- Play call-and-response clapping games using rhythms from the piece:

Dynamics

- Play a G major scale and arpeggio:
  - *pp*, *p*, *mf* and *f*
  - Play the scale with one dynamic ascending and then suddenly change to a different one descending.
- Play call-and-response games using short phrases from the piece, exploring these dynamics.

Aural

- Listen to a performance of *Prelude*.
- Clap the pulse as you listen to the performance, emphasising the strong beat in the bar.
- Discuss the tempo – does it vary at all?

Title, character and context

- Listen to some other preludes.
- Why do composers write preludes?

Articulation and improvisation

- Make up a little piece based on the opening interval of a fifth. If possible, use both hands and experiment with using the pedal.
- Using the notes and rhythm of bar 1 or 3 explore:
  - Slurring
  - *Staccato*
  - Accents
  - Playing the last note with an *sf*.

Introducing the notation (opening the book)

Rhythm

- Set up a suitable pulse in $\frac{2}{4}$. Play two bars (hands separately or together), then count and hear the two bars internally. Play the next two bars and so on.

- Find and clap any recurring rhythmic patterns.

- Tap the rhythm from the notation until secure, hands separately at first and then (section by section) hands together.

Dynamics and articulation

- Make up some phrases that are:
  - *pp* and slurred
  - *mf* and slurred
  - *f* and accented
  - *f* and slurred
  - *mf* and *staccato*

  Find examples of each of these in the music.

- Circle all the dynamics with appropriate colours.

- Compare the articulation of bar 3 with bar 5, and bar 4 with bar 26 (right hand). Discuss all the differences.

Key and scale patterns*

- Discuss the key of the piece and play the related scales and arpeggios regularly. Experiment with using the pedal when playing the arpeggios.

- This piece is written in C but flavoured with G, D, E flat and E majors. Make up some five-finger phrases in each of these keys.

Aural

- Sing back some two-bar phrases from *Prelude* at an appropriate octave.

- Play a phrase from the piece twice. The second time, make a change for the student to identify.

Title, character and context

- What is a (musical) canon? Find the canon in bars 9 and 10. Make up a very simple canon in C major, perhaps based on a scale pattern.

- What is a sequence? Find the sequence in bars 15–16. Try to continue the sequence by beginning the phrase on another set of notes.

- Think of some words to describe the character of the piece.

* For more help with scales and arpeggios, try the C and G major Finger Fitness sections in *Improve your scales!* Grade 2.

Playing and refining the piece

Rhythm and pulse

- Explore playing the piece at different speeds and discuss which sounds best.
- Tap the rhythm of the piece with both hands and the pulse with a foot.

Scales and arpeggios

- Play the scales and arpeggios of any of the keys associated with this piece in a lyrical and *legato* style (as the opening). Also in a cheerful and light style (like bars 5–6) and in a bold style (like bars 25–26).
- Sight-read pieces in any of the related keys.*

Aural

- Regularly try to hear the piece internally – just the rhythm at first, then the melody too.
- Visualise yourself fingering the piece at the same time as hearing it internally.

Articulation and dynamics

- Make up a piece exploring all the dynamics and articulations in this piece. Choose your own style.

Title, character and context

- Make up a story or draw (or find) a picture to fit the piece.
- Compose a prelude using ingredients from this piece.

Performing

- Focus on capturing the changes of mood, articulation and dynamics when playing *Prelude*.
- Try to memorise the piece.
- Perform the whole piece to relatives and friends and/or make a recording.

* For related sight-reading pieces try *Improve Your Sight-reading!* Grade 2.

Student's worksheet

Prelude ingredients

Key signature Written in C major but centred around G major

Other scale patterns A minor

Time signature ²⁄₄

Dynamics *pp p mf f*

Rhythms

Articulation Slurs, *staccato*, *sf*, accents

Character In turn thoughtful, playful, dramatic, bold

Special ingredients Sequences, pedalling, canon, fifths

Form Elements of a rondo

Terms and signs pauses, *rit.*, *a tempo*, ♩ = 76

☐ Explore these ingredients by making up little musical patterns, exercises or phrases. Mix and match them where you can. Tick each ingredient when you've used it.

☐ Write these tonic triads, adding any necessary sharp or flat signs (but no key signature):

G major   D major   A major   C major

☐ Sight-read this piece and list its main ingredients here:

Cheerfully

☐ Add barlines to this rhythm, then clap it and make up a melody to fit the rhythm.

☐ Write out the left-hand notes of the last bar at the same pitch but in the bass clef:

Gachou no Koushin (Kaneda)

All about... high energy, multi-colours and movie-like music

Pre-notation activities

Rhythm

- Choose and clap a suitable pulse in $\frac{2}{4}$, emphasising the first beat of the bar.
- Play call-and-response clapping games using rhythms from the piece:

Aural

- Listen to a performance of *Gachou no Koushin*.
- Clap the pulse as you listen to the performance, emphasising the strong beat in the bar.
- Discuss the dynamics and articulation of the performance.

Key and scale patterns

- Play the scale and arpeggio of C major from notation and from memory.
- Explore elements of D flat major (from the pattern in bar 10).
- Learn and repeat this left-hand pattern:

Make up some energetic right-hand music to play over it.

Dynamics

- Play a C major scale and arpeggio:
  - *mp*, *mf*, *f* and *ff*
  - with a *crescendo* and *diminuendo*
  - with short, vivid *crescendos* and *diminuendos*
  - with the rhythm on each note.

Articulation

- Play some patterns from a C major scale and arpeggio using:
  - *Staccato* and accented *staccato*
  - Accents and *sf* accents
  - on each note.

Title, character and context

- Improvise and/or play call-and-response games in C major, using ingredients from the piece.
- Explore the interval of the minor second. Make up a duet using this interval.
- Discover other pieces about animals.
- Find and listen to other marches for piano.

Introducing the notation (opening the book)

Rhythm

- Set up a suitable pulse in $\frac{2}{4}$. Play two bars (hands separately or together), then count and hear the two bars internally. Play the next two bars and so on.
- Find and clap any recurring rhythmic patterns.
- Tap the rhythm from the notation until secure, hands separately at first and then (section by section) hands together.
- Discuss ties and compare the rhythmic patterns in the left hand bars 1–4 with bars 18–21.

Key and scale patterns*

- Discuss the key of the piece and play the scale and arpeggio regularly.
- Find examples of the music passing through D flat major and E flat major. Make up some patterns in these keys that will help to learn the music.
- Explore the scales and arpeggios of keys related to C major: G major and A minor. Discuss their relationship.

Articulation and phrasing

- Explore the opening four bars, identifying the four different articulation markings and making sure they are played differently.
- Identify the one three-bar phrase in the piece.

Special ingredients

- Study all the two- and three-note chords. Practise them with the various dynamic and articulation markings found in the piece, and then with their own particular markings.
- Explore the left-hand melody (bars 18–25). Then choose one of the two-note right-hand chords from the piece and make up a new left-hand melody to go with it.

Dynamics

- Look at the various dynamic levels in the music and notice how they fit the phrases.
- Circle all the dynamics using different colours for the different levels.

Title, character and context

- Discuss the title.
- Think of some descriptive words that illustrate the character of the piece.

* For more help with scales and arpeggios, try the C major Finger Fitness section in *Improve your scales!* Grade 2.

Playing and refining the piece

Rhythm and pulse

- Explore playing the piece at different speeds and discuss which sounds best.
- Tap the rhythm of the piece with both hands and the pulse with a foot.

Scale and arpeggio

- Play the scales and arpeggios of any of the keys associated with this piece, connecting them with as many dynamic and articulation markings from the music as you can.
- Sight-read pieces in any of the related keys.*

Aural

- Regularly try to hear the piece internally – just the rhythm at first, then the melody too.
- Visualise yourself fingering the piece at the same time as hearing it internally.

Articulation and dynamics

- Every bar in *Gachou no Koushin* has articulation and dynamic markings. Choose various single bars, play them and consider whether the markings are being brought vividly to life.

Title, character and context

- Make up a story or draw (or find) a picture to fit the piece.
- Compose a new *March of the Geese* using ingredients from the piece.

Performing

- Focus on the exaggerated and energetic character when performing *Gachou no Koushin*.
- Try to memorise the piece.
- Perform the whole piece to relatives and friends and/or make a recording.

* For related sight-reading pieces try *Improve Your Sight-reading!* Grade 2.

Student's worksheet

Gachou no Koushin ingredients

Key signature C major

Other scale patterns
D flat major

Time signature $\frac{2}{4}$

Rhythms

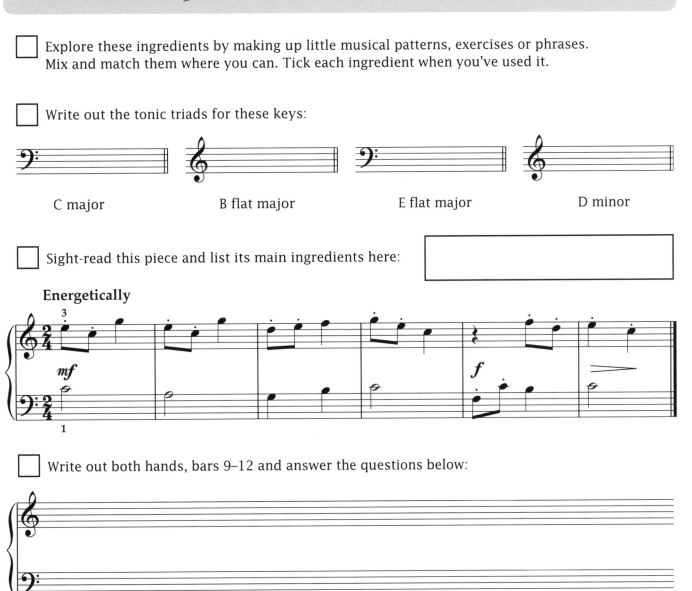

Dynamics *mf f ff*

Articulation *Staccato*,
accents, *sf*, slurs, slur
with dot

Character Quick and lively,
marching geese, forceful,
witty

Special ingredients
Left-hand melody, repeated
notes or chords, seconds
and thirds, sequences

Form Introduction – Ternary-
like – Coda

Terms and signs *Hayaku
genkini*, ♩ = c.108, *sempre
staccato, D.S al Coda*

☐ Explore these ingredients by making up little musical patterns, exercises or phrases.
Mix and match them where you can. Tick each ingredient when you've used it.

☐ Write out the tonic triads for these keys:

C major   B flat major   E flat major   D minor

☐ Sight-read this piece and list its main ingredients here:

Energetically

mf   *f*

☐ Write out both hands, bars 9–12 and answer the questions below:

- Circle or put a bracket over any intervals of a semitone.
- What is the name of the shortest note value here? _____
- What is the lowest right-hand note? _____
- Write in the names of the left-hand notes in bar 12.

Summary

Pre-notation activities

Key and scale patterns

- Get to know the key, scale and broken chord from memory and from notation and explore related keys too.
- Use call-and-response and question-and-answer activities (playing/singing).
- Play the scale and broken chord with the various dynamic levels and the articulation of the music.
- Play the scale and broken chord in the character/style of the music.

Rhythm and pulse

- Clap a pulse in the tempo of the music.
- Explore any new rhythms or those particular to the piece.
- Connect these rhythms with the scale and broken chord.

Character

- Listen to and identify relevant musical features in the music.
- Explore other ingredients or concepts found in the music (such as sequences, ostinato, ornaments, intervals and so on).
- Discuss the title.

Introducing the notation

- Look for recurring patterns. How many times do they appear? Are they always the same or do they vary?
- Look for passages based on scale and broken-chord patterns.
- Discuss the key, scale and triad.
- Make sure all the markings are understood.

Further activities for exploration

- Play the scale and broken chord in the style of the music.
- Discuss and explore related keys.
- Tap the pulse with a foot (or use a metronome) and tap the rhythm of the piece.
- Improvise using different combinations of ingredients.
- Hear passages of the music internally and then sing them.
- Continually connect with short sight-reading pieces that explore similar ingredients.
- Explore the style and composer (through project work that has been researched on the internet or at a library).

Playing and refining the piece

- Regularly hear the piece internally, particularly thinking about a well-controlled and musically shaped performance.
- Develop images, stories, colours or shapes – any imaginative ideas to help give character to the music.
- Regularly play the scale and broken chord and related keys in the style of the piece.
- Compose a little piece using the structure, style and some of the ingredients from the piece.
- Choose a bar or passage and play or sing it at a different pitch (i.e. starting on a different note).
- Make more connections with short sight-reading pieces that include similar ingredients.
- Practise playing through the piece fluently, understanding and interpreting all the markings.
- Perform the piece to family and friends.

Playing the piece with increasing fluency

- Play sections and/or the whole piece at a variety of speeds.
- Play sections and/or the whole piece with a range of dynamics (beyond those marked in the piece).
- Play sections and/or the whole piece with a variety of articulations.
- Hold the notes down with one hand and play the written notation with other.
- Student and teacher play alternate phrases.

Preparing to perform the piece

- Listen to other performances of the piece.
- Record a performance and listen critically.

Use the activities in the following boxes if students need extra work on particular areas.

Scales

Pick and choose from these activities as appropriate

- Identify the key-notes on the keyboard (right and left hands).
- Find the hand position for the first few notes (right and left hands).
- Play the key-note (either hand), hear the first few notes internally and sing those notes. Play the notes.
- Think about the fingering and play a full one-octave version of the scale, broken chord or arpeggio. Then play hands together and more octaves if appropriate.
- Play the pattern upside down! (Descending and then ascending.)

Aural

Pick and choose from these activities as appropriate

- Choose a bar (just one hand or hands together) and hear that bar in your head.
- Play the first note of a scale, broken chord or arpeggio and hear the whole pattern in your head.
- Play a bar (one hand at a time), hear it in your head, and then sing it.
- Play the same bar again and then sing it, changing one note.
- Find a short piano piece online with similar ingredients, listen to it and then describe its features: smooth or detached notes; loud or soft; major or minor; does it change speed?

Pulse and rhythm

Pick and choose from these activities as appropriate

- Clap the pulse of the piece at an appropriate tempo.
- Clap the first beat of the bar and hear the other beats in your head.
- Tap the pulse and with a foot and clap the rhythm of the right and then the left hand.
- Tap the pulse and hear the rhythm of each hand in your head.
- Are there any repeated rhythmic patterns in the piece?
- Tap the rhythm of the left and right hands together.

Reading

Pick and choose from these activities as appropriate

- Choose a bar, set a pulse going, play the first note, try to hear that bar in your head and then play it.
- Play a bar a few times, play it from memory and then write the bar down from memory. Check it is correct!
- Read as much of the piece as possible in your head (in other words, hearing the music internally.)

Improvisation

Pick and choose from these activities as appropriate

- Make up a short piece using just the key-note, but any rhythms from the piece.
- Make up a short piece based on the scale of the music.
- Choose two or three ingredients from the music and make up your own piece.
- Make up your own short piece based on the same title.
- Make up an exercise to practise a tricky bit.

Timeline

Grade 2 composers

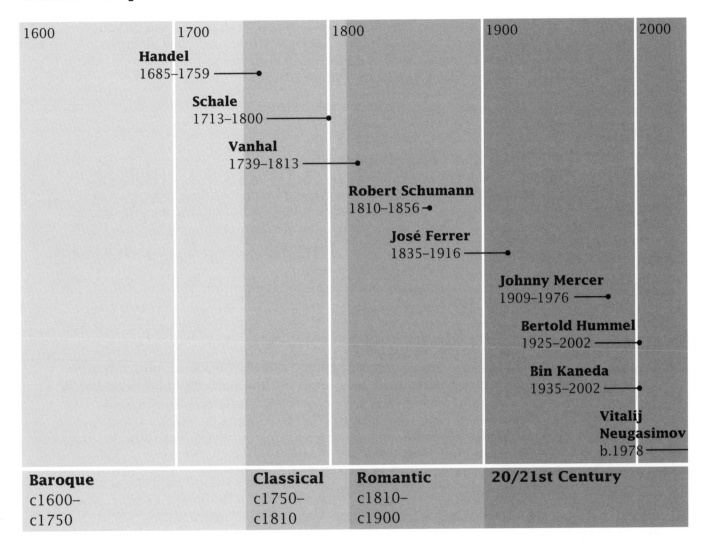

1600	1700		1800	1900	2000

Handel
1685–1759

Schale
1713–1800

Vanhal
1739–1813

Robert Schumann
1810–1856

José Ferrer
1835–1916

Johnny Mercer
1909–1976

Bertold Hummel
1925–2002

Bin Kaneda
1935–2002

**Vitalij
Neugasimov**
b.1978

Baroque
c1600–
c1750

Classical
c1750–
c1810

Romantic
c1810–
c1900

20/21st Century

Also by Paul Harris

Improve your aural!

Designed to take the fear out of aural through fun listening activities, boxes to fill in and practice exercises, these workbooks, each with CD, focus on all the elements of the aural test. A range of interconnected activities are included to help develop the ear, including singing, clapping, playing your instrument, writing music down, improvising and composing. Fulfils all ABRSM exam requirements.

Improve your sight-reading!

This series of workbooks is designed to help overcome sight-reading problems, especially in the context of graded examinations. Step by step players build up a complete picture of each piece, first through rhythmic and melodic exercises, then by the study of prepared pieces with associated questions for the student to answer, and finally with a series of practice tests.

Improve your scales!

Using 'finger fitness' exercises, scale and arpeggio study pieces and simple improvisations, Paul Harris' brilliant method teaches students to know the notes and thus to play scales and arpeggios with real confidence. Forms a solid basis for the learning of repertoire and sight-reading techniques, as well as being invaluable preparation for exams.

Improve your theory!

Covering all the requirements for ABRSM theory exams, these workbooks are firmly rooted in Harris's highly successful *Simultaneous Learning* approach. Learning theory has never been so much fun or seemed so natural! Seamlessly linking theory to pupils' own pieces and utilising aural and compositional skills, these books will transform how theory is learnt and improve every aspect of musicianship.

To buy Faber Music publications or to find out about the full range of titles available please contact your local music retailer or Faber Music sales enquiries:

Faber Music Ltd, Burnt Mill, Elizabeth Way, Harlow CM20 2HX
Tel: +44 (0) 1279 82 89 82   Fax: +44 (0) 1279 82 89 83
sales@fabermusic.com   fabermusicstore.com